Sure Way to Higher Grade Scores

*George H. Ilodi,
D.P.M., Ph.D., F.A.A.F.S.*

**PublishAmerica
Baltimore**

© 2007 by George H. Ilodi, D.P.M., Ph.D., F.A.A.F.S.
All rights reserved. No part of this book may be reproduced, stored in a retrieval system or transmitted in any form or by any means without the prior written permission of the publishers, except by a reviewer who may quote brief passages in a review to be printed in a newspaper, magazine or journal.

First printing

At the specific preference of the author, PublishAmerica allowed this work to remain exactly as the author intended, verbatim, without editorial input.

ISBN: 1-4241-8903-9
PUBLISHED BY PUBLISHAMERICA, LLLP
www.publishamerica.com
Baltimore

Printed in the United States of America

Sure Way to Higher Grade Scores

*George H. Ilodi,
D.P.M., Ph.D., F.A.A.F.S.*

Foreword

More people have supported the completion of this book than I can name, and I wish to express my gratitude to them.

I am also grateful to my children; George Jr., Hamilton, Blessed and Stephanie for their encouragements, understanding and hope.

This manuscript is designed to help those who may want to improve their study styles regarding the subject matter covered. It is written with the understanding that the writer is not engaged in rendering legal, educational or professional advice. If legal advice or other expert assistance is required, the services of a competent professional person should be sought.

Make high grade scores your target by reading and applying what you have and what you learn from this book. Then, when you can handle the challenges of examination, you can focus your potential into success.

—George H. Ilodi, D.P.M., PhD

Dedicated to:

Dominic and Agnes.
George Jr., Hamilton,
Blessed and Stephanie.

Table of Contents

Introduction	13
Good Lecture Notes for Higher Grades	15
Keeping in Touch	18
How to Become Higher-Grade Wise	20
Set and Achieve Higher-Grade Goals	21
Emotional, Physical and Mental Preparations for Higher Grades	25
Study Is Hard Work	28
Defeat Failure Signs	29
Examination Tips	32
Technique of the Problem Course	34
Know Your Grade in Advance	36
Stay Focused	38
Types of Tests	41
Test Making	44
Career Planning	46
Having Fun Studying	48
Communication and Time-Wasting Devices	50
Keeping Tabs on Your Time	52
Summary	55

"A good test is something that is designed to shake you up, so be prepared. It should be something that is less than bad and better than good!"

Introduction

Sure Way to Higher Grade Scores gives you detailed methods on how to score high marks on your examination, if you are a typical student who works hard for your grades. The title of this book has, no doubt, caught your attention. Surely you would like to believe it, but you can't. It may sound very unbelievable because, high grades, for most people are elusive dreams. If it makes sense, or not, why should you work so hard for less than good grades?

You can benefit from my experience now and if you do, you can achieve high grades with minimum effort. Most people believe that it is simply the opposite; more work and study culminate in higher grades. This is not necessarily always the case.

The major key to academic success is concentrating your efforts on the right things at the right time. By using the methods that are outlined in this book, you can, with minimum effort, determine your grade in advance, on any examination or course. You can learn how to save time, have fun studying and plan for your future at the same time.

Let me tell you now from the start, that by following these methods, you can become a master of you fate regarding studies. Therefore, you can determine your future in a way. This may sound like a fantasy, but please know that it may be, but not when carried out well.

You may ask, "Why do my techniques work and how do they work?" The why of my techniques can be seen from various angles: academic, religious, psychological, environmental, metaphysical, and philosophical points of reasoning? The how of my techniques will be found in this book? It is my main objective to show you how to be a master of your grades, how to develop unique, effective and practical techniques that will mean academic success to you forever.

These techniques work. If they worked for me, worked for some of my students who cared to apply themselves to good study habits, then they should work for you. These strategies have been used for several years in my academic work, in my area of research in Laboratory Medicine and in clinical practice. Much earlier in my practice and during my adjunct faculty appointments at colleges in Cleveland, Ohio and surrounding cities, my students used these techniques. Those who benefited from these techniques were the students that gave them a try and stuck with their experimentation of the techniques. Those who practiced my techniques harvested the fruits of their labor.

These techniques were developed by me in response to my desire for academic success. You can call academic success anything you like provided it includes higher grades and excludes failing grades. Having spent much time in the classroom, both as a student, graduate student, podiatric medical student, lecturer, podiatric physician and surgeon, you can bet on my telling you about successful study techniques, note taking, test taking and time saving strategies because this is a statement made from my experience in going through those phases of life. This statement also includes experiences and exchanges of ideas and feedback from my fellow students, friends, patients, clinicians and colleagues.

Good Lecture Notes for Higher Grades

It is absolutely imperative that you are attentive in taking accurate notes during lecture. A good set of lecture notes is one of your most important assets in getting ready for an examination that will guarantee you high grades and eventual success.

If you have the facts in a well-organized format, you are well equipped to do the necessary reviewing, as we shall be dealing with in this book. Some students benefit greatly by rewriting their notes after lecture. If you do this, consult your text, study guide or fellow student for reinforcement and organization. After reviewing your notes, if you do not understand any information, take time to seek assistance early rather than wait until just prior to an examination.

It has been observed that students take notes in a very haphazard style, claiming that they will copy them later. This is a poor technique for two reasons: 1) Usually the notes do not get copied and the originals are not of much use after a few days or weeks have gone by 2) If the notes are copied as I said previously, it is a waste of time in a way. You ask, "Why?" Because they could have just as well been done right in the first place. That is why.

A few "DO NOT s" for your guide:

- Do not try to take down everything the lecturer says. All lecturers tend to repeat a great deal, but you simply need to write it down once.
- Do not take down the first thing the lecturer says on any topic because it is probably introductory material. Listen for signals.

- Do not try to use outline form. You will only get bogged down in listening and trying to understand. Underline the first main topic. Then write down in list form, but without numbers, the most important things the lecturer talks about.
- Do not try to make sub-topics and sub-sub-topics. Keep following the LIST and UNDERLINE format until something else. Then you will know that it is time for another main topic.
- Leave wide margins and do not crowd your lines together. Abbreviate and use short forms as much as possible. Do not bother to write complete sentences.

Good Note Tips:

- The notes should be such that they indicate the main points of the lecture.
- The notes must show the relationship of the details to the main points and must include enough illustrative details, if any, to enrich the content of the lecture.
- The notes must be neat and attractive in appearance.

The tips here on note taking do not have to be complied with if you have already devised other methods that are working and yielding higher grade dividend for you. You should realize that the manner of lecture presentation also come into play. Power point, over head, blackboard, transparencies, broad-cast, web cast, other web based and computerized classroom management systems of presentations also take on other creative approaches one may want to be familiar with.

In case you have to miss a day or so of class, you must try to cover yourself. Get the full name and phone numbers of at least two classmates. Write them down on something you won't lose. There are modern technological devices from some electronic stores that can also help you with note taking if it is better to take your own notes than to rely upon someone else's note second-hand. Some students may also attend any of the other sessions of the same course by the same instructor if that instructor allowed it. They try to get the information they missed. It is like attending a lecture twice. Believe it or not, some students have tried it. Furthermore, they raised their test scores and grades by doing so.

Keeping in Touch

In working towards high-grade scores, it is highly important to also network or to keep in touch. There are many ways one can network or keep in touch. Let us assume that one is in a classroom for lecture. It is very easy to start networking with the person you are sitting next to.

You do not necessarily have to know the person, or like the person either. All you have to do is to assume responsibility for your success. You have to assume the responsibility for your high-grade score. All these rest within you. Any opportunity you have to exercise those inner powers, by all means do it. Going back to the person sitting next to you in the lecture room, all you have to do is introduce yourself, pick up a brief conversation, and get a brief idea about the individual during an interlude. If your gut feeling directs you to proceed then go ahead for the next step, which is about the lecture. Get to have the feel of where the person is coming from, how the person feels about the lecture. If you feel you should continue with the inquiry then by all means proceed. If you feel you should discontinue, again by all means do. The aim of even making contact with the person next to you in the lecture is to see if you could develop a contact, a networking system. If that was a warm, prospective positive contact then nurture it and keep it. If you should have concerns or should require anything in the future, you sure have a contact. If you missed a lecture for some legitimate reasons, at least you have some source to go to. You should make it a habit of developing contacts in lectures. These sources of contacts can become invaluable should the need arise. You can use this technique to develop such contacts. In developing this networking connections, gender and other social considerations play lesser role. Your goal is for success and high grades. In a course, if you can develop two to three networks; those should help you scale over hurdles in times of need. In some instances, you may not need the benefits of networking to achieve your goal in the course. These net workings are simply back up plans. If the instructor is accessible; which most are, then by all means make sure you can maximally utilize all the necessary help you can get by going directly to the instructor for any information you may need, miss or want clarified. People, who use my techniques of networking, find it helpful because they pay particular attention to the basic integrity of relationships and the basic subject matter. We all know that responsibility manifests in successful student study outcome. These students make the grade. The whole personality in each case is about grades. Good grades are who they are. They don't manufacture excuses! People who are good at manufacturing excuses are never good at making good grades. These other set of people will come up with excuses before you ask. If the weather is bad, you have buttered their bread. That was probably why they missed the test. That was probably why they did not take notes. That was probably why they did not go to the computer room. This shows that responsible attitude to the lecture at hand is highly indispensable to higher grade score

How to Become High-Grade Wise

Do you know what it means to be high-grade wise? Are you test wise? If you can answer these, then go to the next section in this book. But if you are not sure, continue reading. You are test wise when you have some understanding of how to go about answering the various types of questions that are on any examination. For example, what techniques would you use in answering essay questions? What techniques would you use in answering multiple-choice questions? What techniques would you use in answering true-false, matching, fill-in-the-blank, multiple-of-multiple, oral or even practical exams?

How might these techniques differ from one another? You are higher grade wise or test wise when you have the skills or techniques of tackling various types of questions. How do you acquire the skills? Of course you must have knowledge of the subject in order to do well on any test or examination. However, it depends upon how you answer the questions. Even if you have full knowledge of the subject matter, you may sometimes do poorly because of the manner in which you tackle various test items. The bottom line lies in setting up and achieving your study goals so you can become higher grade wise.

We shall soon be dealing with my practical study techniques that correlate with guaranteed higher grades.

Set and Achieve Higher-Grade Goals

Here are some tips that will help you to prepare emotionally for test by setting up and achieving your study goals towards higher grades. You need goals not only in life, but also in your study so that you know where you are heading in the process of achieving higher grades and in the process of educating yourself. As soon as you know what you want to achieve, you can set your mind to it, achieve it and stop worrying about whether or not you will do well in courses. Setting goals is one of the strongest ways of motivating yourself to study efficiently and effectively.

You MUST, repeats MUST, write your goals down on paper; not in your head. It was noticed from interviews conducted with my former students that those who did not set specific study goals were usually uncertain about what they had to do, and when they had to do it, in order to pass their course. Therefore, you should know that if you can determine what you should study to pass a course and set up a schedule to achieve study goals, you should be in good shape. The next question is how do you figure out what your study goals should be? What are the sources of information for the course? Who can tell me what to do to pass the course? You can get the answers in this book! Some of the best sources of the information include, but are not limited to: your brains, your fellow students, your instructor, your homework, course syllabus, course outcomes and objectives, course schedules, course requirements, class discussions, student manuals, programs, course policies, old notes, old test papers, class notes, class tapes, electronic databases, electronic course reserve, course web page, software, simulations, laboratory equipment and other instructional technologies that may be indicated. From these various sources, you will be able to know what is demanded of you in order to pass the course and achieve a higher grade. This way you can become a more intelligent person about the test material.

How do you know how to set your goals? First you must know from the beginning of the course what the course demands in terms of task performance. Generally, course tasks require minimum passing grades, completing some projects, writing papers, passing quizzes, passing written tests, practical exams, presentations, class participation, attendance and other academic requirements the instructor may stipulate. It is imperative that you know where, when and how these tasks should be accomplished in addition to knowing the types of tasks that you must accomplish to attain a higher grade.

Remember that at the beginning of this section, you were told that you must write your goal down on a piece of paper. Let us use the goal of achieving higher grade in an exam. The first thing we do is to write it down as we have just done. The next step will be meeting the schedule that will achieve the goal. The next thing is to determine how many chapters or units of activities that must be studied between now and the exam. We then determine the sources of the test questions. We then determine when and where the exam will be and the materials that it will cover. We then plan to spend specific study periods each week generating test questions from course notes, old tests, discussion groups, and friends and so on. If the text has test bank, that can also be a good resource to use. We then plan to spend specific study periods each week making and taking practice tests. We must know how we are doing by watching our progress. This may look tedious, and complicated and not as easy as clicking on the computer icon. Well, there is a lot of work involved in being successful in school. Is there an easier way? Sure, there are many ways of doing things. Some students "cram". That is, they wait until the day before the exam and what happens is that they spend half of the night trying to memorize facts which may have little meaning to them. This is hardly the best way of setting up and achieving your goals for higher grades and academic success. Waiting till the last moment is like giving a beating on the stomach and the fingers. The gastroenterologists and neurologists will not be very pleased with you. This goes like the old saying of "plan your work, work your plan." Besides, this technique of scheduling and meeting your study goal will help to prepare you mentally, physically and emotionally—an added advantage to your higher grade experience.

The technique I just described took me years to develop. Why was it developed? The answer is simple. It was my desire for academic success. We will not go into the technical meaning of academic success. Simply take it to mean achieving higher grades in academic courses or better still, passing grades that exclude failing grades.

During my undergraduate years at the State University of New York at Buffalo, it took me over a year to get over not only culture shock, but also a different type of educational system from the one in which my earlier education was derived. My first semester grades were marginally above survival in the non science courses, even though my academic load was more than recommended. To get into medical school, you have to keep straight A's. Realizing that most of my course mates were also brilliant and, more importantly, many of them Americans – were better prepared to handle the course work, that is, take notes; take examinations, study and record lecture. I thought I was more knowledgeable than they were in terms of the course material; it became obvious to me that a fast and drastic solution was needed in my academic progress, or else my academic career could have been in oblivion.

What you need to realize is that in this book, we are dealing with academic success that is the index of higher grade. We all know that after exams, students complain of an unfair exam, some complain that someone else did better academically, who either did not study much or did not know the material well enough, or is not that brilliant. Most of these complaints are justified. The most brilliant or the" smartest" people in a particular course do not always achieve the highest grades. At the same time, the students with the highest grades are not the hardest workers or even the best at understanding the course material, you will surely agree with me. Therefore, this book will show you how to achieve higher grades. You must know after reading this book that it is to your advantage to achieve the "best" which is the highest grade possible for the minimum amount of effort.

Emotional, Physical and Mental Preparations for Higher Grades

Before we continue, let us look back to the emotional, physical and mental levels of higher grade scores in tests.

Emotional Preparation:
One of the best ways to prepare emotionally is to have confidence in your ability to handle the test. We are not speaking of a false confidence, but one that it based on earnest and hard work through study and preparation. You should learn to accept the test for what it is and should be concerned about the test; not worried. Worry causes mental stress that wastes energy and cuts down on your ability to perform well. If you begin to worry about the examination that you will have to take, you will not be able to keep your mind on preparing yourself. Too much worry can actually lead to failure. The opposite attitude, or the "I don't care about the test anyway" can be equally serious. The wise student will try to discover his weaknesses, and work to strengthen them in preparation for a test. The better prepared the students are, the more self-confidence the students will have when the tests are taken…

You need to have confidence in yourself and in your ability to pass the test. The person who has confidence in himself will do much better than one who lacks this faith. Your confidence should be based on knowledge or belief that you are qualified with regard to what will be asked for in the test. You should get rid of strong emotional feelings about tests. A good test is something designed to shake you up, so be prepared. It should be something that is "lesser of bad and better of good!" It may even give you the opportunity to demonstrate your competence and ability. You will be better off going for the exam rather than trying to "skip" with the hope that you will be able to take a make-up test. Naturally, there are times and circumstances under which it is not possible to attend school .Here it is something that cannot be avoided. Some times some students prefer to "Cut" examination, thinking that they are not prepared, or that they can do better on "make-up tests." I think that people who take make-ups usually score much lower than students who take their tests on time or earlier. So, if you have attended classes regularly and have kept up with your work with a reasonable degree of success, there is little reason to be fearful, upset, or worse, be emotionally troubled over a test.

Physical Preparation:
This does not mean that you should go to your primary care physician for a physical examination. One of the best prescriptions here is a good sleep at night. If you have to come to school with bloodshot eyes covered up by sunglasses, you had better not expect to do well on the test.

Physiologically, the mind and the body are dependent upon each other for proper function.

Some Do's:

- You should provide yourself with the best possible conditions for studying. Avoid areas where you will be exposed to distractions.
- You should be comfortable with your surroundings so that you can involve yourself in intense concentration.
- You should therefore have a place of study.
- You should use the same study area each day.
- You should get yourself into the study frame of mind. You should get right down to work and concentrate on what you are doing.

Remember that if you are tired, you will not be able to think clearly because a test is designed to get at your mental abilities. You cannot accept this challenge if you are tired. While studying, do not strain your eyes.

If you overwork your eyes, you may get headaches, feel dizzy and become nervous. The best way to rest your eyes after intensive reading is to close them for a few moments, or to gaze into the distance. Your study schedule should have a break period. Such a break period should be short and should allow you to relax, to get up and stretch from your sitting position, and not to remain rigid.

Exercise serves to stimulate the digestive and circulatory systems and to prevent tiredness. This helps to keep you in shape and enables you to perform your study in an efficient manner.

Sleep is also important because it helps to restore strength to perform daily tasks. The amount of sleep necessary varies with the individual. The average adult needs about eight hours of sleep. One way to get a good night's sleep is to go to bed at the same time each night. You should develop your own physical preparation and follow it. Too much eating or drinking milk can be sedatives, even though not suggested.

Mental Preparation:

Mental preparation requires study. Study should not be drudge, but an interesting and satisfying experience. Some students dread study because they do not know how to study. Some of the computer generations dread studying. Some of these may prefer clicking on the computer instead of studying text books. A good study method should be concerned about the concepts of the subject. You must then be able to understand these ideas quickly. When you have an understanding of the important facts and ideas, you should be able to remember them. A good study method should enable you to review efficiently for examinations. What is the good study method? A good study method is what you will derive from this book.

Study Is Hard Work

The study methods described in this book, like everything worthwhile, require work and practice. We have just received some general ideas on study habits. We should then realize that there are no short cuts, but that there are ways to study effectively without wasting time and effort. If we use the following method, we will learn to study in an organized and systematic way.

In the beginning, we will learn that this method takes time and effort. However, we may make changes necessary to suit our own study needs. It is a useful system, so to speak. Our job is to make the system work for you. It also requires some discipline on your part, but the dividend in better scores and increased knowledge and confidence far outweighs most other study techniques we might have heard or tried. This is not scientific, but from personal observations and experiences.

Defeat Failure Signs

You must defeat failure signs before success can come your way. In the domain of clinical psychology, positive reinforcement is a term used to describe a condition in which an individual is mentally conditioned to accepting the fat that he or she is defiant in certain mental areas. In other words, reinforcement increases the probability of a response when the reinforcement is contingent on the response. The opposite, which is negative reinforcement, tries to feed back a negative action based upon the premise that the person performing the negative action inherited it or that such negative action runs in the family. These are both failure precipitates because one is already a failure or that one never does well and that such and such runs in the family. Therefore, it should be so with "such and such a person." All these are irrelevant. The point of the matter is that these should not be so.

Sometimes the subconscious and the conscious levels of metaphysical planes may have been under attack. What does this mean? It simply means that the student with the negative reinforcement consistently wants to be acting in a certain way or believes that he or she can only do "so-so." This is at the conscious level of thought. The sure way is to remove the fear of always doing "so-so" in tests, change the attitude on the mind and make much more positive and efficient use of the mind. Then the obstacle of always doing "so-so" which is deeply rooted in the subconscious level will be phased out and replaced with doing super on tests.

One thing that this has suggested now is what is called "self-analysis." We have all heard this thousand of times. Self-analysis is related with the ability to know the "self." This means the perception of one's being, or in other words the "self-image." If one sees oneself as a grade "A" student, one tends to be conditioned in working for the grade of "A", and when one sees self as a "C" student, one tends to do mediocre work. Who wants to be mediocre? To the graveyard with mediocrity. If one sees oneself as inadequate, then that is a poor self-image. This is nothing to be ashamed of because this self-image was already conditioned during the early childhood days by a host of outside environmental factors like classrooms, homes, church and the community where we live. People expect you to be in such and such a way.

In the chapter *Set and Achieve Higher Grade Goals*, a step-by-step outline of what to do to set some goals for study habits have been provided for you. Now we will add what we need to change self-image. In order to do this, we have to change our way of thinking. For us to change our ways of thinking so that we can get higher grades, we must set goals. If we do not set any goal, we will not achieve anything. This is like going to the bank manager to borrow money. The bank manager has to know what we will do with the money, and, of course, how we will pay it back with interest. Of course other things might be involved, but those are trivial.

By the same token, we must set goals for higher test scores or higher grades. In other words, we must know the grades we want in the test way in advance before the test. This is the grade goal setting strategy. Without this goal setting strategy, our chances of excelling in a particular examination are questionable. The point is that we must know our grades because we can only perform at the level or frequency at which we tune our self-images. Once we set our goals by knowing the grades we want, then our performance levels and self-images resonate. The goals we set will determine our achievement levels. Our performances, which will generate our results—which are our grades—are dependent upon the self-image we have projected. This is true! This book will show us how to fight hard, change our situations and change things for the better.

The next thing is to free ourselves of fear and build confidence by writing our goals on pieces of paper. Every day we must look at our goals. Let's say you want a superior grade in a course rather than an inferior grade. First, write the grade and try to ingrain it in your subconscious mind. As soon as you are able to convince your subconscious mind of your superior grade, then through your goal setting strategy, you work towards it but keep it to yourself. Remember not to reveal your goal to anybody because of humiliations, frustrations and other undesirable feedback.

Examination Tips

If you know the past questions for the course, then that is a plus. If you can write the questions for that same course, that is an added advantage, too. Your main concern for doing well in an examination is to know what the questions are. You will discover a technique of knowing the questions for test in advance, as well as having a thorough grasp of the subject matter of the test. In some schools, fraternal bodies become sources of storage of old tests. With modern technologies, most texts have test banks, websites or CD's containing test questions. Some instructors have sites for test banks and review questions. Please try to avail yourself of these resources. This is like a revision method for a test only. If you belong to any of these, you may want to explore the possibility. If you took good lecture notes for higher grades, then you will have no problem putting the little pieces together. After the notes are taken, you must review each note soon after the lecture. Keeping current on learning the material is essential in achieving a good grade.

Remember that establishing a set time to study each day is an integral part of developing good study habits. The sooner the material is reviewed after it is given, the better the rate of retention. You must do periodic review of the materials in the lecture. You should develop formulas, concepts, outlines, mnemonics, graphs and other steps needed to make study meaningful. Self-questioning and answering is one of the most important review processes that you can benefit from. It is helpful to frequently write a term so as to establish a mental impression of that word and its meaning.

Two or more individuals can get together for a review; not only before an examination, but even after the examination. When a term is exchanged with a study mate or a term is repeatedly spoken, retention is improved. Studying with another person helps you identify weaknesses or inconsistencies in your notes. This type of study is most effective. However, prepare first as suggested in this book, and then meet for serious study.

Do not forget to bring all the materials you may need to take a test, such as a pen, pencil, erasers, rulers, slide rule, wrist watch, examination number or admission ticket, identification materials, passport, driver's license, college ID or other ID you might have. Do not forget to bring a tissue. Make yourself comfortable! Come to the test hall neat, clean and in comfortable clothes. You must be early for the exam. You can not afford to be late . A good idea would be to check out the hall way before the examination day to make sure that you know where it is. In short, dress modestly and be comfortable.

As soon as questions are distributed, get down to work. Make a survey. Look over the test. If there are any directions being read, be sure to listen carefully. Some people like to answer the easy questions first and then the more difficult questions last. Some people go by the page, which one you are comfortable with, use it.

Technique of the Problem Course

For those of us who are students, it is presumed that academic domain is a common place. Students attend lectures, discussions, seminars and the rest of them. In these meeting, handouts are probably given and notes are taken. The goal at these meetings is to understand whatever information the lecturer has to deliver. If notes are given, then one does not have to take down everything that the lecturer says. Power point notes can be helpful some times. All one has to do is put down the important facts and ideas. This could be supplemented by extra readings. But all these notes and readings are meaningless unless one has to put them together. As discussed earlier, you must:

1. Put all the notes and readings into one organized unit.
2. Have a general idea of what the lecture is all about.
3. Review the notes after organizing it.
4. Add new information from lectures. After two to five lectures, review note from previous lecture.
5. Review the notes again.
6. Make any outline of the notes after the additions.
7. Study the notes and the outlines.
8. After new lectures, say 2 to 4, and then do another addition of new information.
9. Review the notes.
10. Make detailed outlines.
11. Review the notes and the outlines.

12. Make up questions from the outlines.
13. Try to answer the questions.

If you can follow this systematic process, you are actually achieving the main goal of the technique of the problem course. The key point is an indirect production of the lecture material in your own words, and at the same time testing yourself from the material from which the lecturer is going to test you. In all probability, you are pulling all your test questions from the detailed outline which contains the lecturer's examination questions. So you are selecting your questions from the same "gene pool" as the lecturer. That means that you know what the lecturer wants. This is the key to higher-grade scores.

Know Your Grade in Advance

Let me start you with a word that is very familiar to most of you. The type "A" student has school and personal performance demands always at peaks. The type "A" student is mostly a classic over-achiever. The type "A" student is the one that does everything with intensity, from extra-credit assignment to daily routines. The type "A" student wins awards for being conscientious, and is a top notch. This type of student fulfills the old admonition, "If you want to get anything done, ask a busy person. Many type "A" students will not accept a "B" grade. These students are already hard enough on themselves without reading this book on performance. These type "A" students build their whole identities on performances. How well they perform is who they are. By the same token, how well you practice the techniques of problem courses determines how good your grade will be. That in turn determines who you are. We are not saying you should be type "A" student. Rather, by following the technique of the problem course and reviewing, outlining, re-reviewing and making test questions, reviewing again, the study mechanics is being accomplished. You will discover that by following my technique, writing down the grade you want to get in a particular course on a piece of paper, like "A", what you are really doing is making the power of the subconscious work for you. By making notes, reviewing, outlining and testing, you are in a way ordering the conscious to relay to the subconscious. This is one of the "Whys?" you were told at the beginning of this book that my technique may be visualized from various angles. This is from a metaphysical aspect.

Now that you know what grade you desire to get in the test and by following my technique of problem course to the point of self-examination by testing, the next thing is self-analysis. Self-analysis is done through re-examination of the weak areas in the test score, if any. If after the test, you find that there are some areas where you are weak, this is the time to review again and re-examine yourself. You have to put conscious effort into any problem area you may have after which you can then let go consciously. My experience shows that sample examinations taken a day or so before the actual test day is better than the one taken days ahead of the actual test day. After the final sample test, then review your weak points and your outlines, up until the day of the exam. If you have been following my technique, you find that you need not actually do any work on the exam day unless you really want to because all these days the study has been on the roll and the subconscious has been put to task. All that is left on the actual test day is for you to unlock the subconscious.

This technique is a suggested way to high-grades. It needs a lot of hard work. If you are not willing to work hard then you are going to harvest nothing. But, if you are willing to put in a few hours a day, then it is a goldmine for your dream grade harvest. What do most exams have in common? The answer is that most exams are testing your ability to answer questions correctly. Since you already know how to do this from my technique, what is left is for you to prove yourself.

Remember that different lines of studies are slightly different. So you should not be dogmatic in your approach with some courses because some require a slightly different approach. For example, in a course on computer programming, of course you need a computer machine to prepare for the course; a course like chemistry, you need to do some more writing and a course like mathematics, you need to solve problems; not just reading the text. So, practice solving the problems. This is really what is meant by not being dogmatic in you approach. The technique is mechanically applicable to almost any course. My student who used the techniques had dramatic changes in their grades in various courses, not just in Biological sciences and Chemistry, but also in others.

Stay Focused

I have observed many highly talented, smart, hardworking, brilliant people go through school with mediocre grades. One could ask, what was the problem? What was going on or how could that be? I had written on goal setting and high grade score in the previous sections of this book. I stated that from the interview conducted that those students that failed to set specific study goals were not sure where they were going or how to get to where they thought they were going. That meant how to pass the course successfully without fault. It is vital to stay focused on your primary objective of the lecture; be it art or science. In the previous chapter I had explained step by step how to accomplish your goal, how to set and achieve higher grade goals. You were given the steps to make commitment into chasing your higher grade score. You can stay focused on your set goal, just as long as you have the determination and the zest for that. How do you keep the determination and the zest? Again, the previous sections on setting and achieving higher grade goals enumerated those steps. You know naturally that we humans tend to avoid pain. We always look for the easiest way out. That is why at the beginning of this section, I stated that the most talented and the smartest hardworking people sometimes end up with mediocre grade. They try to avoid pain. This is the key. They want the easy way out. They end up making little progress. They want to avoid the trouble, care, effort and due diligence often required to accomplish something good. These sets of people are very capable and able as I said but putting the effort becomes enigmatic so to say, to make the act become a reality. This is like some one trying to lose weight like yesterday, not today or tomorrow. This is like someone trying to buy a second vacation home this year not even next year. This is like somebody trying to stop smoking but can not have the time to accomplish it. This is like some one trying to go to the professional school, like medicine, law, nursing, engineering, architecture, pharmacy and the list goes on and on but did not have time to finish. Nothing comes easy. These sets of goals require time to accomplish them. They require time, planning, methodology, patience, and hard work to bring them into reality. Thus staying focused on goal has been used by me, some of my students as well as others to achieve better grade score and also accomplish tasks.

At the beginning of the term; I would like each person to write down the expected grade on a course on paper. This you will also write at a visible secret sport for yourself. I tell them it does not mean that that the grade you write will be handed over to you. I tell them, the grade they write also belongs to them; they can take it or refuse to take it. The grade you write will help you stay focused on your course towards higher grade score.

The next thing is that they have to focus on "large terms," "high grades," big thinking. They have to list ways of accomplishing the focused goals. In most cases, with the ways our minds work, the ways of achieving the goals always come in various forms. The greatest book of all time-The Holy Bible; the New Testament sections even taught us how to set our goals in large terms. You get what you ask for. This means whatever you ask for, you get; if your mind earnestly desires it and if you put your mind, effort, energy and time to it. Those studying time and human mind know that out mind only knows of now. To stay focused on your goal you have to start working on your goal now not tomorrow not next week.

Your focused goal has to be realistic. If you set a goal you know you may not achieve may be because of your background, then you will be defeating yourself in a way. Let's take, for example, a course on a high level math. If someone who never took even high school math, never was interested in math, never solved math problems and just never made the effort but put down a grade of "A" in a high level math. With the same level of mental attitude towards math, one would be bamboozled on how this person is going to get this "A". You can see that the goal does not seem realistic but it is not impossible either. The only real thing is that it will be a long shot. This is like an uphill event trying to capture the "A" grade.

The next step will be putting your focused goal in the "now" form, that is the present form of the event. If you like, you can use the English form-present form of a verb. When we put a focused goal in the present form, that is the present time, it becomes very potent. What it does in the mind is to press the mind into action. This is a psychological process that turns ideas into reality. I will get an "A" grade and ways and means of meeting the goal begin to manifest. All of a sudden I will begin acting like an "A" student even though it has not manifested but looks as though it has already manifested. A lot of us use it all the time without realizing what we are actually doing.

The next step is concentrating in large terms as far as the goal is involved. Think in large terms. Think big. Don't think small. Don't think "C" or "D". Think "A" or "B", mostly think A++. This means we are what we think. This means the way we conceive our idea, talk about our idea and act our idea will eventually determine the velocity by which we accomplish our focused goal in a given direction of high grade score. For three semesters I noted that most students ended up with the grades they put down. So this technique works. I have not conducted a big study; this was just a pilot study. With these steps in mind, there is no doubt that the momentum for you to scale the high grade will prepare you for even higher grades than expected.

Types of Tests

Objectives Tests:
Objective tests may be of the multiple-choice type, true-false, completion or matching. In taking these tests, you should budget your time properly. A good technique is to divide your time into three equal parts. In the first period of time, you should read over all of the questions quickly. Answer the easy ones first. In the second period, go back to the questions which you left unanswered. If you have a hunch or a reasonable guess, go to it. Otherwise, it is best to avoid wild guessing. In the third period you will be able to go over the blank question in a more leisurely manner. You will have more time to consider the items and thereby avoid wild guessing. If there is no penalty for guessing, then go ahead and guess and make sure you put down something for every question. The question of guessing should not arise if you have been following my practical technique of problem course because by the time of the examination, you are already armed with adequate knowledge.

Essay Tests:
You need to look over all the questions in essay tests. You need to know quality point allocated to each question by the instructor. Looking over an essay test is like reading a menu in a restaurant because you want to know the prices. You want to spend the amount of time that is relative to the quality of points allocated to a particular question. After the survey, do the easiest ones first. You should be

specific. There should be no long story that is beating about the bush. Dabble into the question and do what it requires of you.

Here are some terms you will probably meet in an essay type exam:

1. Compare: State the similarities and differences of two or more subjects.
2. Define: Tell about the characteristics and qualities of the item. Synonyms and antonyms may help.
3. Describe: Include the finer points of the subject under discussion.
4. Illustrate: Describe using comparison, analogies, and examples.
5. Relate: Show the connection between two or more subjects.
6. Trace: Show the history, development and progress of the subject under discussion. Give specific dates and events leading to conclusion.
7. Analyze: Show the essential features of the subject, rather than an overview.
8. Explain: You need to present facts to convince the examiner and that is all to it.

These are some of the terms used in essay test. When you know what is expected, you can keep to the point and not go off track describing and explaining things which do not actually answer the questions. You should look for key words such as those described.

When you understand the question, you may want to make a quick and brief outline. Do not waste your time making a pretty outline! Do it on scratch paper. You can then check your outline against the question to see if the answer will be good enough. Then write your answer out in full. Do not forget to budget your time! Don't spend half of your time on the first question and then try to rush through the others. In fact, one of the most common faults of students in essay tests is the poor use of time. These special types are for essay examinations:

- Determine the length of the test
- Allow time for each section and still get to cover the entire test

- Determine which questions carry the most points and allow more time for them
- Estimate the difficulty of the questions and answer the easy ones first
- Check your work for clarity, completeness, accuracy, style and appearance

For special papers, term papers, extra credits, other write ups where the work is done outside the classroom; it would be a good idea to put the paper in a good looking plastic cover.

For the special written type of work or project that is done outside the classroom within a time frame, always note the due date and time. By the same format, organize your material, and work on it checking for typos and the rest of it. When you are done you may want to put the finished work in a plastic folder for hand in .It looks more professional and more presentable in plastic protecting folder. In the eyes of humans, things that seem to look better may mean better value which may translate into higher grade score. If the content of the paper has substance, that is an added plus in terms of grade score.

Test Making

If you can understand the question, it is a lot easier to do well in an examination. So let us see how some questions are made. Let us start with the multiple-choice.

Multiple Choices:
The most common type of test question is the multiple-choice. In this question, the answers are already given. You must decide which answer is correct. You must choose the best response to the question. Sometimes the directions ask you for the most likely or the least likely. You may be asked which of the following is correct. You see how important it is to read and understand the directions. Usually a multiple-choice question presents a statement followed by several possible answers. Sometimes you are asked to give the best answer. At other times you will have to use your judgment and select a best answer or best reason in an answer to a statement. Look out for such catchwords as always, never, sometimes. Remember that extremes are usually not the correct answer. Be on the lookout for those choices which are fairly close in meaning. When you read a multiple-choice question, you should look at all of the choices first. A good technique would be to cross out the letter of number in front of the choices which are surely wrong. This should narrow your choices down to one or two possibilities and increase your chances of a correct answer. You must make sure that you read all of the choices because the last one may state "all of the above" or "none of the above." If you took the first answer, you may be wrong.

True-False:

Quite often the true-false question is used on an objective type test. The true-false questions are like the multiple-choice except that you have only two choices instead of four or five. Again, as in multiple-choice test, you must be on the look out for words likes instead of four or five. Again, as in multiple-choice test, you must be on the look out for words like always, never, and sometimes. Always and never usually make the statement false.

A good method in working on true-false items is to answer those you know first. If you are not sure about an item, but have a hunch, mark it lightly with your pencil and go onto the next item. After you have finished all the questions, you can go back to those you marked lightly. This will give you extra time to consider your first response after you have completed the entire section.

Matching Questions:

In matching questions, there are two columns. You are asked to match items in one column with items in the other. Here are a few ways in which you can handle matching questions. Work from one list only. You should take each item in the left column, one at a time, and search the list in the right column, looking for the proper match. As you complete each item in the left-hand column, cross it out so that it will not distract you in your later selections. Another way is to run a line from each item in the left column to its corresponding match in the right column.

Career Planning

Studies show that, those with defined goals most likely succeed than those with undefined goals. Why invest all these efforts into achieving high grades if not for career planning. In all these high grade scoring systems; the end result is to have a career. As one is applying these techniques of problem solving towards high-grade scores, at the back of the mind should be a place, and that place should be career planning.

As one is succeeding, one should be thinking of vocation and avocation with both open minds. Sometimes peoples' avocation turn into their vocation and sometimes peoples' vocation turn into their avocation. Regardless of what or how they turn out or did not turn out, knowing that these successful grades can become meaningful occupations can become catalytic in making both ends meet. You can see that high grade scores and occupation are mutually exclusive. Because of this, career planning should be an integral part of your successful academic goal. There are many sources one can go to for career planning. Schools, colleges, universities and other designated websites and places have career planning and counseling preparations in place. One should avail themselves of these helpful resources in planning for successful life. Remember that in most cases, the best thing to do in this situation would be to seek out advisers to help make these career plans. One should gather as much information as possible regarding career and after gathering the information, then one can take the necessary leaps of faith which the high grades have helped put one through. You should remember that this is your life, as I used to tell my students. Here you should pound on the table, meaning that you measure the distance you want to go or you anticipate before you leap. You want to be sure. You do not want to take chances. You want to be deliberate with every move you make because it is your life! You must do you your homework well before you go act. There is no rush because your career is one of the most important decisions you will have to make in life. Your calculated efforts are not procrastination on your part; in this case as you know, but wise cautious approaches that have no comparison so to speak

Having Fun Studying

This has been a term that comes up every now and then in everyday conversations. Can one have fun preparing for higher grade score? The answer is a resounding "yes". With all these techniques for higher grade score, if one is not careful, probably one may even fall in love with the techniques and get too serious and reduce the spontaneity of the fun. Acquisition of knowledge is interesting and can be full of fun. The techniques in this book are full of fun. When the good grade is presented, it can be pleasurable in a way. As I said, acquisition of knowledge is interesting and can be full of fun. It can also be challenging but with patience, practice, preparation, diligence, and faith the challenge can be surmounted because you have been presented with the opportunity in this book .On the other hand, and in some occasions, the trials of failing can in most times present themselves as successes in disguise. Failure comes in different angles. Regardless of the manner, it should always be viewed as a lesson for improvement. If failure was due to unnecessary fun play, then one needed to reexamine self and change and device some creative strategies for good. But if failure was due to not having fun in studying, it was probably because having fun was driving you overly serious. Having fun is enjoying these techniques, having high grades, not being too serious with yourself, having sense of humor. Having fun is also having the capacity to be funny and not get tensed up. You are having fun practicing these techniques of higher grade score if you can remain very objective and keep your perspective. You know surgeons are technical people in an away. Imagine how a patient will feel if a podiatric surgeon were to perform a delicate podiatric operation and gets tensed up and not having fun doing it. You can bet the hypothetical patient may even jump out of the surgical table. Enjoy this book, get serious, and get the most out of it. What I am saying is that you should get all you can from this book to improve your lot while you enjoy it without losing your perspective and objectivity. This is my philosophical meaning of having fun reading this book.

Communication and Time-Wasting Devices

I would rather use this term loosely because I had previously written about some distractions earlier on in this book. Laptops, computers, cell phones, video games, T.V, and other communication devices can play central role in learning and in improving our grade scores. However some of these if not well guided can be time consuming and time wasting rather than being the useful means through useful communication. The amount of critical thinking involved in using these devices is still debatable. One thing for sure is that some of these devices can help one stay focused, think, and concentrate while others can help in causing complete waste of time and complete loss of attention. T.V viewing and these other adverse behaviors like music, violence, aggression, imitation, and commercial are greatly time consuming. T.V viewing can be a way the viewer is potentially whiling away productive hours and therefore preventing active learning of these techniques. Most of the commercials are nonintellectual and do not provide opportunity for the viewer to seek this self improvement opportunity. There are few intellectual and educational activities in the television. The next time killer is cell phone. Cell phone is good technology. People, who know how to use cell phone, use it wisely and use it for what it should be used for. The problem with some of these cell phones is that they can become time consuming devices. Some people waste too much time talking on the cell phone that sometime one wonders what they are really talking about. Some keep talking and keep running up their meter that by the time the bill makes it in the mail box; they notice they exceeded their budget. If they could direct the time, effort and energy they invested in cell phone talking into better grade preparation, I think the benefit in the later will outweigh the loss time and dollar in the former. Sometimes it is noted that some people communicate with cell phone in the classroom for one thing or another. Those are highly disruptive and time consuming acts that undermine the time that could be invested into prioritizing for high-grade score. Some other communication devices have their own time consuming, learning advantages and disadvantages. Where do these communication and time wasting devices come in? They come under time. It is surprising that some times people ask for time without knowing that they have the time, and that they kill the time as they have it. They keep wondering where they are going to get the time to study. The answer will be found on how to manage time in this book.

Keeping Tabs on Your Time

The last section on time wasting communication devices actually led us to look into this precious commodity called time that is vital in achieving our high-grade score. One of my favorite scientists dealt with this idea of time. Albert Einstein (1879-1955). He won a Nobel Prize in physics in1921 and was best known for his elaborate theories of relativity and the quantum theory of radiant heat energy. In sum according to Einstein, time and distance are relative. With this in mind, we see that time is everything according to Einstein. Time is life. Time is money. Time is now. Time is high grade scores.

In the realm of time, you can see that we do not have much of it. As time comes; so you must watch it. If you fail to watch and use time efficiently, you will always be in conflict with your plans. Remember that you can not add or take out a second out of a twenty-four hour block that has been allocated to a day. I hear students complain every now and then about not having enough time to study. We have been blessed with twenty four hours in one day. There is a lot of time in one day for one to actually plan and accomplish whatever one intends to achieve in that day. It is a fact that people are busy always doing something and as I said earlier on if you are too busy to get things done, remember that there are others who are even more busy than you, who can get more things done than you can imagine and you complain of not having enough time to study. The point I am making is that there is enough time. The only sets that have no time are those sets in eternity with infinite time line .Human beings have time. Try to use your time wisely and effectively. If you think your killer time is cell phone, turn it off and focus on your high grade earning techniques. As we noted before, time is life, if you want to waste your life, waste time. Time is high grade scores. If you want to earn poor grades, waste your time on irrelevant things. It is that simple. Who is in charge of your life? Philosophically your answer may be "God". God has given you the will to make choices. It then follows that you are personally responsible for your time. You are in control of your life and time by free choice. You are in control of your high grade score by free choice. I would suggest some of the common sense ideas we all know and use that may help us use time effectively. Some of these time savers are:

1. Set your watch 5 minutes fast (that's what I do)
2. Work smarter and harder
3. Plan your work and work your plan for high grades.
4. Prioritize your tasks. Do the most important things first and the least important last that have to do with you achieving high grade scores.
5. Concentrate your efforts on scoring big grade.
6. Think positive with time and higher grade score.
7. Think time conscious with higher grade score.
8. Don't sleep too much. If you sleep too much you are really sleeping away your life and reducing your chances of achieving the higher grade score.
9. Do not waste your time thinking of any poor grade in the past, and regretting.
10. Always make time to do things that will lead to scoring high grades. You can have "to do list." It helps with organization.
11. Do not watch T.V if you can, except the intellectually challenging programs.
12. Mind seriously how you use the time on the cell phone.
13. Seek the advice of professionals, when in doubt about any of the methods on your career planning.
14. Mind the type of friends you keep; that have no bearing to improving your grade.
15. Set deadlines on lectures and materials

16. Plan your financial affaires well and live within budget. Cut your coat to your size. Financial stress can interfere with focusing on achieving higher grade score.
17. Think of creative approaches towards time savings always; regarding means of achieving higher grade score.
18. Think and act present (now), not later towards higher grade scoring techniques.

Summary

You now have specific guidelines about practical ways to organize your time and energies for successful learning. These include, but are not limited to, self-weekly schedules, outline of a specific study plan for each course, tests, reviews, and the techniques of the problem course. In addition, keeping in touch, career planning, remaining focused on your goal and having fun while managing your time effectively are areas of immense value to high grade score. High grade scores are like a linear equation. Where high grade scores are equal to preparations plus the techniques in this book.

My experience was that these techniques enabled me to know my grades in advance, and in most cases, my guesses were better than top percent on any examination than expected. If you practice these techniques, you will realize that the rewards in terms of achieving high scores will be proportional to your commitment to achieving these goals. I wish you success and happiness in realizing your unique potential by practicing and applying these techniques of higher grade scores.

Printed in the United States
88951LV00005B/571-633/A